Using Floppy Disks with the BBC Microcomputer

Using Floppy Disks with the BBC Microcomputer

Keith Davis

Third Edition

A Cumana Publication

Published by
Cumana Ltd,
Unit 1, The Pines Trading Estate,
Broad Street, Guildford,
Surrey GU3 3BH, England

First published March 1983.
Second Edition published June 1983.
Third Edition published November 1983.
Fourth Edition published May 1984.

British Library Cataloguing in Publication Data

Davis, Keith
  Using floppy disks with the BBC microcomputer.—3rd rev.ed.
  1. BBC microcomputer   2. Floppy disks (Computer storage devices)
  I. Title
  001.64'42   QA76.8.B3

ISBN 0 9508762 3 2

Typeset by FD Graphics, Fleet, Hants.
Printed and bound by Clark Constable,
Edinburgh, London, Melbourne.

Preface

The aim of this book is to introduce the newcomer and novice alike, through simple stages, to the relative complexity of the floppy disk drive. Particular attention is paid to the environment of the BBC Micro within which they work. It is felt that by taking you first through the jungle of mystery that surrounds floppy disk drives and then expanding on this theme we can then include a complete guided tour of the BBC Disk Filing System (DFS) to give you a better understanding of what is available to you when you purchase the DFS for the BBC Micro.

As all good books, we start at the beginning and look at the floppy drive and its terminology. We unravel the confusion of some of the terms applied to Mini Floppy Drives. We then go on to a step by step guide to connecting the drives to the computer and running your first programmes.

From there we move to the other facilities offered to the disk user and give a complete summary of the DFS commands and how to use them.

We end with the disk filing system and some useful hints and tips.

No attempt has been made to describe anything beyond the simple stage and therefore no great knowledge is required to understand the contents and become reasonably proficient in the use of the DFS and its commands.

In the second edition I added two more chapters, extensively rewrote the section on Random Access Files with lots of programming examples and extended the Error Code Section. With this third edition, the emphasis of the book is changed to slimline drives.

Keith Davis. October 1983.

Contents

Chapter 1
Introduction to Data Storage

This Book has been written with the newcomer in mind and is based around the B.B.C. Model "B" Microcomputer with Disk Interface.

There are a number of different data storage devices that are needed for the efficient operation of all computers whether they be large scale main frames or micro computers. There is the ROM or Read Only Memory, this holds fixed data which cannot be altered. This data is usually the program which holds the BASIC interpreter. It also tells the microprocessor how to look after such things as keyboard entry and how to handle the data. Then there is the RAM or Random Access Memory, this usually holds the current running program and its variables. As the name implies, data can be stored or retrieved in a number of ways. Programs are normally loaded into the RAM area as they are needed. When a new program is required it is loaded into the same RAM area and overwrites the old stored program. It can only hold data whilst the computer is switched on and running. As soon as the computer is turned off then all data and programs in the RAM are lost and only that data which is fixed into the ROM is kept. There are other types of memory whereby the program data and files can be downloaded before turning the computer off. One of these is the punched tape, on which most of the early computers used to store and load their programs. Punched tape again holds fixed information and it cannot practically be altered. Then there is magnetic tape. This type of storage media has the advantage that data can be stored onto magnetic tape and filed away. The data on the tape can also be changed when required to hold a new program. It has several advantages over the punched tape. With a Personal Computer this convenience extends to being able to use a normal cassette recorder for long term storage and retrieval of programs and data.

Faster Access

Whether you have just started in computing or have had the use of a Micro for some time, sooner or later you will come to feel that the use of a tape recorder to save and retrieve programs can become frustrating. Initially, this tape recorder was just fine and allowed you to save and retrieve your brand new programs. But now you have a larger collection of software and find yourself spending rather a long time searching for the latest version of your Home Management package. This normally happens when your program library grows to an extent whereby finding a particular program halfway down a tape is a time consuming business. This seems especially true just as you want to show a friend your latest masterpiece of programming power.

It is at this point that you begin to wish you had bought a better storage and retrieval system. This is where the Floppy disk drive fits the bill so nicely. With data transfer rates a couple of hundred times faster than cassette. Improved reliability in loading and saving programs and a "Catalogue" of diskette contents available to you in a few seconds rather than several minutes.

With the cost of Floppy disk drives now within the reach of most Micro owners and the promise of lower prices to come, it seems only right that we try to de-mystify the operation and facilities offered by a typical disk based system and its associated D.F.S. (Short for Disk Filing System).

Chapter 2
The Floppy Drive

Figure 2.1 shows a typical Floppy disk drive and the following points should be noted:–
(a) Indicator lamp illuminates to show that the drive is active and busy.
(b) Drive facia and slot for inserting floppy diskette.
(c) Lever for locking diskette into the drive. This lever is normally closed across the slot after inserting the diskette. It engages the hub or clutch of the drive into the hole of the floppy diskette. Note the way the diskette is fitted into the drive. The diskette label is uppermost and on the rear edge. The small notch on the left is the write protect notch and if covered by a small adhesive tab will prevent the drive electronics from storing information onto the diskette. This is useful if you wish to avoid accidental erasure of certain diskette data.

Figure 2.1. Floppy Disk Drive.

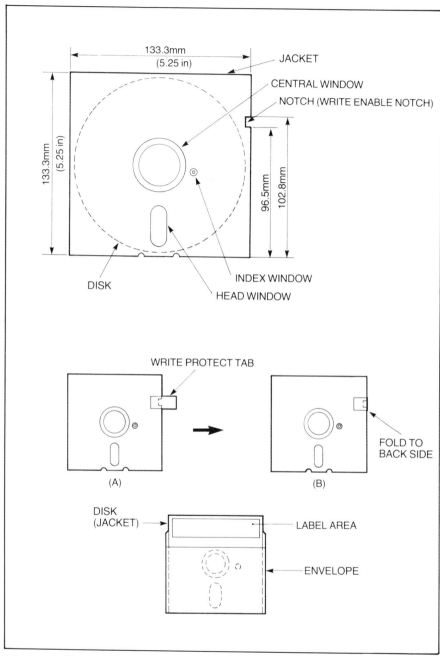

Figure 2.2. Typical Floppy Disk.

See Figure 2.2 for explanation of the floppy diskette.

(d) Control cable. This carries the signals needed to operate the drive. It is through this cable that all communication between the disk drive and the computer are carried out. It must be inserted the correct way round. If the cable is reversed then normally this will result in the drive motor and electronics staying permanently in the "ON" condition. If a diskette is in the drive at that time then one or more of the tracks will be totally erased.

(e) Power cable. This must be fitted to an approved type of plug with an earth connection. If in any doubt then always consult a qualified person.

(f) ON/OFF switch. It is normal practice to power all external devices prior to applying power to the computer. Always wait till the entire system is powered before inserting a diskette into the drive and be sure to remove it before switching anything in the system OFF.

Standards

There are two normal standards for 5¼'' disk drive capacity. These are 40 track and 80 track drives. The only difference between 40 and 80 track drives of the same make are internal and transparent to the user. The 40 track drive lays down its magnetic tracks at a pitch of 48 tracks per inch or as is commonly known 48 TPI, whilst the 80 track drives lay down the tracks at 96 TPI, exactly half the track width of the 40 track drive. Both 40 and 80 track disk drives are available with a single head (which records on one side of the diskette only) or with a double head which will record on both sides of the diskette. A double sided drive is specified as having twice the storage capacity of the equivalent single sided disk drive.

The Diskette

When a diskette is first used it has to be Formatted. This is a program that lays down magnetic circular tracks onto the diskette and then segments each circle into a number of sectors. See Figure 2.3. Each one of these sectors has space to store 256 bytes of information. In the case of the B.B.C. Micro which only operates in the SINGLE DENSITY mode, it lays down 10 sectors per track. That is equal to a storage area of 2,560 bytes on each track. Therefore a 40 track drive will have a formatted capacity of 40 times 2,560 or 102,400 byte storage area. As two of these sectors are reserved for the catalogue a total of 101,888 bytes are available for program storage. The storage area available on an 80 track drive, less the catalogue, is equal to 204,288 bytes.

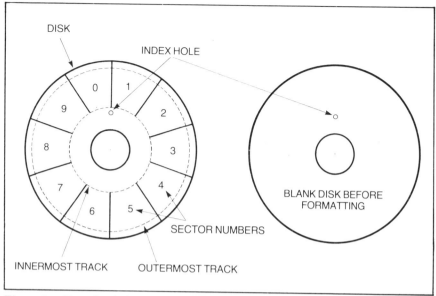

Figure 2.3. How the disk surface is laid out after format.

For the sake of convenience the drives for the B.B.C. Micro are normally given their capacity to the nearest 100k. Therefore a 40 track single sided drive is quoted as being 100k capacity whilst the 80 track single sided drive is quoted as being 200k and finally the 80 track double sided is known as a 400k drive. These figures are assuming single units. If the drives are in a dual packaged unit then the above figures are doubled.

Density and Capacity

Note that the above calculations are made for single sided SINGLE DENSITY 40 or 80 track. The 80 track drive is simply a higher capacity drive. The recording density remains the same. Even if the user goes to double sided drives, the B.B.C. Micro is only capable of reading and writing in SINGLE DENSITY. To imply double density means that the number of sectors per track has been increased from say 10 sectors per track to 18 or 20 sectors per track. It therefore follows that each track will hold twice the amount of data. Typically 4,608 bytes per track. It is a common mistake to think that double density implies double the amount of tracks. It is the host computer that decides which density it will operate in. Most of todays modern floppy disk drives will handle either density and no setting has to be done by the user. It is a function completely controlled inside the computer.

First Sectors

As mentioned above, two of the sectors are used for the catalogue. This catalogue is allocated sector zero and sector one of the very first track. Note: the convention of using zero for the first item is a valid notation. When a program, or file as it is more commonly called, is 'saved' to a floppy drive then an automatic catalogue entry is made with the file name that was given to it. This entry contains the track number and the sector where the computer can find the start of the file. Secondly it contains the number of sectors that the computer has to read to load the complete file into its memory. The Disk Filing System looks after the Disk drive and is able to find all spare consecutive sectors on a diskette when it is required to store a file. It does this by moving the Read/Write head via a stepping motor inwards and outwards across the rotating diskette. On a single sided disk drive the Read/Write head normally operates on the underside of the diskette. Whilst on a double sided drive both sides of the diskette are used. No user intervention is required when saving or loading files from a floppy disk drive. Certainly there is no rewind or setting to record as would be found on a cassette tape storage system.

Ground Rules

The type of floppy diskette used on the B.B.C. Micro is more commonly known as a mini-floppy. This is a 5¼ inch diskette made from a mylar coated circular disk enclosed in a stiff cardboard sleeve. The mylar coated diskette rotates inside the sleeve at 300 RPM.

Each box of diskettes normally comes with a set of diagramatic instructions of what to do and what not to do. Here are a few Do's and Don'ts. Never write on the diskette sleeve or label attached to the sleeve. Always mark up the label BEFORE placing it on the diskette sleeve. Never place the diskette within any magnetic field like a loudspeaker, mains transformer, moving coil meter etc or anything that you suspect to be magnetic or that could otherwise damage your diskettes.

When the diskette is not in use or in the drive, return it to its protective jacket. Never leave an unprotected diskette on any surface where it might pick up damaging particles of dust or grit. Grit in particular can cause serious damage to the precision Read/Write head used in the drive. Avoid excessive bending of the diskettes and if possible keep them in the rigid plastic diskette holders that can be obtained from most computer shops. Do not touch the exposed recording surface of the diskette. Finally do take care to keep your diskettes away from excessive heat or cold.

In selecting the right type of diskette to use always choose a branded type of diskette that is certified for the number of tracks that you wish to use them on. Users of 80 track drives can expect to pay slightly more for certified 77/80 track diskettes. If you change from 40 to 80 track drives at any time then do not expect all your 40 track diskettes to work error-free in the 80 track drives.

If one of your diskettes get damaged in any way either physically or magnetically then try to copy the files of that diskette one at a time onto a known good formatted diskette. You should at least save most of your files and only those in the damaged area will be lost. If you have any really valuable software then it is up to you to keep backup copies of those diskettes in a safe place.

Instructions on formatting, copying and backup are given elsewhere in this book.

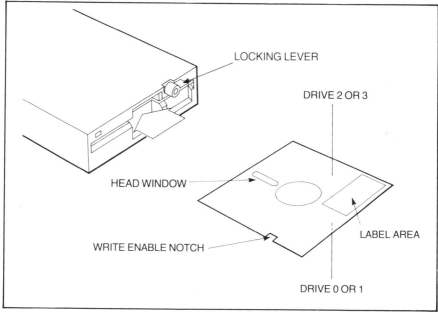

Figure 2.4. Insertion of the disk.

Chapter 3
Setting up

Now that we have had a brief look at the disk drive it is time to connect it to the host computer. In this case it is the B.B.C. Model "B" computer fitted with the disk interface. Firstly, check that your drive or drives are addressed correctly as drive 0 and drive 1. This addressing can be checked in the case of Cumana drives by removing the drive cover and looking at the link settings that are located towards the rear centre of the drive electronics PCB. These drives are made by TEC and do not employ a head load solenoid. Reference to Chapter 14 will give details of setting up drives that have a head load solenoid.

The following links should be made (connected) for drive 0. This is normally called the boot drive, the link marked DS0. On a dual unit the second drive will have the link DS1 made. All other links should be unmade or left unconnected. See Figure 3.3 for TEC drive link settings.

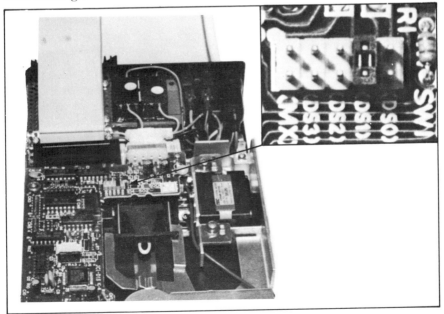

Figure 3.1. Locating the links on a TEC drive.

Other types

Other types of drives use a similar convention and the guidelines given for the Cumana drives should help you get the correct settings even if the drive uses links that have to be cut. Don't forget that if the links are mounted in a DIL socket then it is quite easy to change the links for a DIL switch.

The termination

A final check should be made on the termination resistor pack. This looks something like a small integrated circuit and in the case of the Cumana drives is normally black in colour and is mounted in a DIL socket. It sometimes has the word BECKMAN written on it. Other terminating resistors that you may meet are the type which look like lumps of shiny black plastic, again mounted in a DIL package so that it can be unplugged. There should only be one terminating resistor fitted to the drive assembly whether you have one or two drives. If you have a dual drive assembly and each drive has one of these resistor packs then remove the resistor pack from the drive that will be closest to the computer leaving the resistor pack in the drive that will be on the end of the cable.

The drive cable

Normally all Cumana drives come already set up to use but should you have any reason to either add a second drive to the system or fit the cable yourself then it is quite easy to do. It is a 34 way ribbon cable with three connectors on it. Two of these connectors are close to each other at one end and are of the edge connector type. Fit the end edge connector into the drive with the cable coming away from the bottom of the connector. In the case of a single drive it is necessary to bring the unused connector back to the outside of the case as there is little room inside. With the dual drive fit the remaining edge connector to the other drive ensuring that the orientation of the cable is kept the same. A red line runs alongside one edge of the cable to assist in this. There is a groove at the back of the drive housing where the cable may rest in as it exits out. When the lid is refitted to the assembly you will find that the cable is not crushed by the lid.

Plug into the Micro

Now fit the other end of the cable to the B.B.C. Micro as illustrated on

10

page 11. The cable is fitted to the underside of the machine and connects onto the outlet marked Disc Drive. This is a 34 way header type of outlet and care must be taken when fitting the plug onto it. It is possible to mis-align the connector and damage the header. Make sure there are no bent pins on the outlet and if a locating key is fitted then use this to centralise the connector. When the cable is fitted correctly then it will exit downwards from the connector and flow towards the rear of the Micro (Figure 3.2). Having successfully connected the drive to the Micro it is now time to test it out.

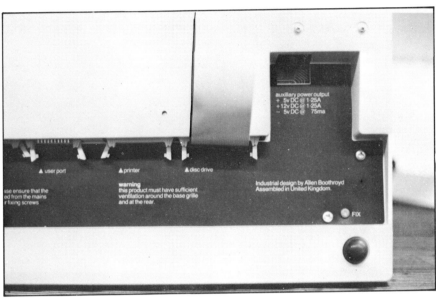

Figure 3.2. Connecting the Drive Cable to the Micro.

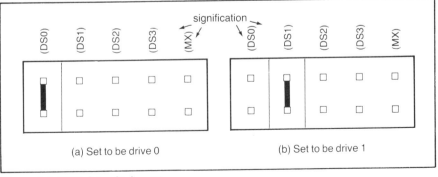

Figure 3.3. TEC drive link settings.

Chapter 4
Switching on

First check that all the power to all units in the system is disconnected. Next connect the mains lead from the disk drive assembly into a recommended AC mains outlet and turn the outlet ON. Locate the mains switch at the rear of the drive and in the case of the Cumana drive turn the switch ON to apply the power to the drive/s. The switch will illuminate to indicate that the drive/s are powered. There should be no response yet from any device. If however the drive/s start up then do check that the connecting cable is the correct way round. If the drive/s stop rotating when the connector is removed from the Micro then both the connectors on the drives need to be reversed. If the drives of a dual system still rotate after removing the Micro connector then only one of the drive connectors are reversed. In either case DO REMOVE the power before attempting to correct the plugs. It is also possible for the drives to rotate on their own if no terminating resistor is fitted.

Startup

Assuming that you have applied power to the drive/s and all is well then you may proceed to apply power to the B.B.C. Micro. After it is switched on you should press the CTRL & BREAK keys together. This should result in the following display on the CRT of the monitor.

BBC Computer 32K
Acorn DFS
BASIC
>

Another message may appear in place of the BASIC if you have one of the special software ROMS fitted but the initialization sequence is completed when the bottom cursor prompt > is displayed. Before checking out the disk drive/s for the first time it is advisable to place a small adhesive tab over the write protect notch alongside the lefthand edge of the utility diskette. It is also recommended to have a few new unused diskettes ready to be formatted and make a backup master.

Booting

Place the Utility diskette (supplied by Acorn) into the drive or in the case of a dual drive into the drive allocated drive 0. Press both the SHIFT and BREAK keys firmly together and then release the BREAK key first before releasing the SHIFT key. Assuming the auto start option is set then this should have the effect of running the auto !BOOT program on the diskette. At the moment this is a program that describes the main utilities available on the master diskette. Pressing SPACE BAR will then run the program that draws the B.B.C. Owl logo and plays a number of notes. At this point you can decide if you want to continue with the demonstration programs or you can press BREAK to return to the startup message. Indeed the only way you can get out of the demonstration programs is to press the BREAK key.

See Appendix 1 for making your own utility diskette.

Disk command

You may now try your first disk command to the computer and ask it to give you a list or CATALOGUE of the diskette contents. To do this type in the following ★CAT and then press return. The drive/s should start up and after a second or so should display a list of the diskette contents. There is a full syntax for all commands and the one for catalogue is ★CAT <DRV> where the option in the <> markers may be omitted and a default value will be used. In the case of DRV a value of 0,1,2 or 3 may be used. An example would be ★CAT 1. This would catalogue drive 1. At this stage we can continue to the format procedure. If you have 40 track drive/s then use ★FORM40 below or for 80 track drive/s use ★FORM80.

If you have only one drive then use procedure 1/ but if you have two drives then use procedure 2/.

The BBC Format routine is given first and then the Cumana Format Routine. Whilst both these programs operate differently they both achieve exactly the same result.

BBC Formatter

Before commencing format you should save any basic program that is in the machine as the formatter program will use part of the basic work area.

1/ Type in the following command and follow it by pressing the RETURN key.

★FORM40 0 (or ★FORM80 0).

14

The computer should respond with a message similar to this:–

Are you sure you want to format drive 0?

DO NOT answer this yet. Remove the utility diskette and put in one of the diskettes to be formatted. Then answer the prompt with a Y. As soon as you have done this the disk drive will start up and proceed to format the diskette ready for use. A display on the screen indicates which track it is formatting and if it cannot verify any tracks then it will display the track number (in hexadecimal) along with a question mark. 11? would indicate that it was unable to verify track 11 hexadecimal which is track 17 decimal. If you make any mistakes in answering the prompts then you will have to replace the utility diskette into the drive and start over again.

At the end of the format routine you are asked if you want to format again. Put another blank diskette into the drive and answer the prompt with a Y. You will then be asked for the drive number which is 0. And finally again it will ask are you sure you wish to format that diskette. The procedure is the same for any other diskettes that you might wish to format. When you have enough formatted diskettes then you should answer the end of format question with an N and replace the utility diskette into the drive. It will then be necessary to reset HIMEM by pressing the break key.

Two drives

2/ For a dual drive system the utility diskette can remain on drive 0. Simply type in the following command line followed by the RETURN key.

★FORM40 1 (or ★FORM80 1)

The computer should respond with a message similar to this:–

Are you sure you want to format drive 1?

At this stage put one of the diskettes to be formatted into drive 1. Then answer the prompt with a Y. As soon as you have done this the disk drive will start up and proceed to format the diskette ready for use. A display on the screen indicates which track it is formatting and if it cannot verify any tracks then it will display the track number (in hexadecimal) along with a question mark. 11? would indicate that was unable to verify track 11 hexadecimal which is track 17 decimal. If you make any mistakes in answering the prompts then you will have to start over again.

At the end of the format routine you are asked if you want to format again. Put another blank diskette into drive 1 and answer the prompt with a Y. You will then be asked for the drive number which is 1. And finally again it will ask are you sure you wish to format that diskette. The procedure is the same for any other diskettes that you might wish to format. When you have enough formatted diskettes then you should answer the end of format question with an N. It will then be necessary to reset HIMEM by pressing the break key.

Cumana formatter

The Cumana Formatter uses sound to indicate track status as it formats a diskette. If you are lucky enough to have the latter O.S. 1.2. then you have the option to turn the sound OFF. Should you wish the sound to be turned off then simply type the command ★FX210,1 before calling up the format program. This will have the effect of turning the speaker OFF. To turn the speaker ON again type the command ★FX210,0.

The command to format a diskette using the Cumana Format routine is exactly the same as the B.B.C. counterpart. Simply type the command ★FORM40 for a forty track diskette or ★FORM80 is you have the eighty track version. You can also specify the drive to be formatted within the command line. ★FORM40 1 or ★FORM80 1.

The screen will blank for a moment after which it will display the Cumana name and version number along with a central diagram.

The Cumana disk formatter uses a triangle pattern which is a graphical representation of a segment of the diskette. The left hand side represents track zero whilst the further right you go towards the tapered end represents the centre of the diskette. You will see that the triangle has numbered vertical lines, each of which correspond to the tracks of the diskette. There are 40 lines for a forty track diskette and 80 lines for the 80 track diskette.

If you did not specify the drive to be formatted within the command line then the bottom line of the display will read:—

On which drive do you wish to format?

This should be answered with a valid drive number between 0 and 3. If it is drive 0 that you wish to Format then please remember to take the Cumana Formatter diskette out before proceeding. After you have entered the drive number, or if it was included in the command line, a test will be done on the diskette to be formatted. If the diskette is found to be blank then the formatter will automatically proceed with the format. If the formatter detects that the diskette contains

16

data or that it is already formatted then the message:–

Disk already formatted. Are you sure?

Will be displayed.

This is to remind you to check that you are indeed only formatting the correct diskette and not one full of your valuable accounting package. Enter a 'Y' to continue or an 'N' to abort the Format.

As the format progresses each of the vertical lines, which represent the tracks, in the triangle will be filled in. If you have a colour display then you will see that the lines are filled in with a Green colour for each successful track. This is also accompanied by a bleep from the speaker.

The formatter will retry up to ten times to verify the track it is formatting. If the formatter made any retries during track verification, this is indicated by the vertical line representing that track being coloured Yellow. Also, the note for that track will be mixed with white noise thus giving an audible warning. This would indicate that the diskette is not to be trusted and could possibly lose data.

If the formatter could not verify the track at all then the track is coloured Red. This would indicate that the diskette is useless and must not be used.

As the track count increases in the display so the pitch of the bleep will increase. If the diskette formats correctly then the end of the format will be signalled by the first two bars of Beethoven's Fifth symphony being played.

If the format failed then this will be signalled by bars from the Funeral March being played. The bottom of the display will also read:–

Fatal formatting error on disk.

At the successful completion of format the option to repeat the routine will be displayed.

Formatting complete.
Do you wish to format another disk?

Simply answer with a 'Y' or 'N'.

After format it will be necessary to restore HIMEM by pressing the break key.

Backup

Having now got a number of formatted diskettes ready for use it is time to make a Backup of the master utility diskette. Again the procedure is different for single and dual drives.

For the single disk drive make sure that the master diskette to be backed up has a write protect tab fixed to it so that no accidental erasure will take place should the diskettes get mixed up. Type in the two following command lines terminating each line with the RETURN key. If you make any errors then you will have to start again at the very first command.

★ENABLE
★BACKUP 0 0

The program will prompt you to alternatively insert the source and destination diskette. If however you have a dual drive then simply place the source or master into drive 0 and the destination diskette into drive 1. Type in the following command lines ending each one with RETURN.

★ENABLE
★BACKUP 0 1

The source is your master or utility diskette that you wish to make a backup copy of. The destination diskette is the formatted diskette that you wish to put the copy onto. If you type in the Backup command without first enabling it you will get the error message:–

Not Enabled.

After the backup is complete it would be advisable to store the master away in a safe place and use the backup master for normal everyday use. Good practice will ensure that you keep two backup copies of your master diskette. Write the diskette name onto the disk labels before you put them onto the diskettes.

Chapter 5
Other devices

Having now made a couple of Backup masters it would be well worthwhile marking them with a number or letter to be able to identify one diskette from another. This is especially true if you have a diskette for example, that you have been using during the daytime and wish to back up the days work before turning the system off. Using a numbering system will also allow you to keep an index of your diskettes and therefore a simple reference to this index will tell you which diskette is required. This saves a lot of time going through each diskette in turn and getting the "CATALOGUE" to find which diskette is needed.

Other routes

Before we move on the available commands on the B.B.C. DFS it should be remembered that the Micro powers up in the DFS mode. Any chaining or saving of programs will automatically be routed to the disk drive. If you wish to load any files from your cassette recorder you must first issue the command ★TAPE. This will then route all loads and saves to the cassette port at 1200 Baud. To return to the DFS system type the command ★DISC or ★DISK either spelling is acceptable.

Other input devices may be used instead of the Tape or Disc and these are normally systems supplied in ROM. Some of these are as follows:

★TELESOFT. For loading Prestel and Teletext software.
★ROM. The ROM cartridge system.
★NET. This is for the Econet system.

If you wish to use a different tape Baud rate then extra commands are available thus:–

★TAPE3. Sets to tape I/O at 300 Baud.
★TAPE12. This is the default 1200 Baud.
★TAPE. This is also 1200 Baud.

More utilities

The Acorn utilities diskette normally has a couple of extra programs besides the FORM40 & FORM80. These are the VERIFY & DCONV programs. The VERIFY program is intended to be a Diskette Read error checking program. What it does is to read each and every sector on each track just to check that all sectors are indeed readable and that no damage has been sustained by the diskette.

DCONV

The other program DCONV is designed to be a transfer medium for those users who have software on the Acorn Atom disk format. This program whilst it will allow a B.B.C. diskette program to be read on the Acorn Atom, does not patch the program. Therefore it may be necessary to patch the program manually before it will run correctly on the Atom.

Drive sides

The B.B.C. Micro DFS can handle up to two physical single sided drives or two double sided drives. With single sided drives the first drive on the system is allocated drive 0 whilst the second is drive 1. With double sided drives however this is still true with the following additions. The second side of the first drive is allocated drive 2 and the second side of the other drive is allocated drive 3. To summarize, on double sided drives we will have drive 0 and drive 2 on the first drive with drive 1 and drive 3 on the other. See Figure 2.4 page 8.

20

Chapter 6
Filespecs

Just as each of the programs you have or had on tape has its own unique name to identify it so the same is true for the disk system. The program name is more commonly known as the filespec. This filespec can be up to 7 characters long and can include digits as well as letters. The following characters enclosed in brackets are, however, reserved for special meanings and should not be part of the filename.

(# ★ . :)

Directory

As explained earlier when a program is 'SAVED' it is given a name. This name is recorded into the 'CATALOGUE' of the disk together with the information on where it is stored. If you wish the file to go to a particular drive then you must include the drive number in the save command. Each diskette catalogue can be divided into a number of different directories with the default being $. Figure 6.1 shows a typical catalogue display and we can describe each section of it here.

```
★CAT 0
UTILITY (nn)
Drive :0                    Option: 3 (EXEC)
Directory :0.$              Library :0.$

    ! B                        !BOOT      L
    DCONV      L               FORM40     L
    FORM80     L               LANDER     L
    VERIFY     L               content

    A.CLOCK                    B.INDEX
    W.ALPHA                    W.BATBALL
    W.BIO                      W.BIORTHM
    W.BPART2                   W.CALC
```

Figure 6.1.

Catalogue

After the command ★CAT was typed in it produced the catalogue as shown. The first part of the catalogue is the diskette name. In this case it is called Utility. The next line shows the drive number and we can see that it is drive 0 (or :0). Opposite this is the option setting. This is set by the ★OPT 4 X whereby X is a value from 0 to 3. As we can see number 3 is (EXEC). On the next line is given the current directory of the drive. In this case it is the $ directory which is the default directory if no other is selected. Opposite this is the current library and drive and directory. Again this is shown to be the default drive 0 (:0) and library .$.

Library

Under this heading come the the files listed in alphabetical order with the current library displayed first.

The first two files are the files used in the auto boot and the 'L' alongside the filename means that it is locked against overwriting. As can be seen most of the important files on the diskette are locked. The files may be locked or unlocked using the ★ACCESS command.

Chapter 7
Using the Filing System & DFS Commands

The Disk Filing System (DFS) used in the B.B.C. Micro is fixed inside a ROM or Read Only Memory. As we said at the start of this book the data stored in a ROM is fixed and cannot be altered. This means that it is always there and your DFS commands are never lost. It has the advantage over other types of disk systems in that it requires less of the Random Access Memory to carry out its commands and programs can usually remain in memory whilst a DFS command is being carried out. There are a few exceptions to this and the Format and Backup routines are just two of them. The others are ★COMPACT, ★COPY and ★LOAD. It is always advisable to SAVE any program that you may be running before attempting to Backup, Format or run any of the other few routines that could destroy the Random Access Memory (RAM). This is because these routines can overwrite part of the program area. The Format routine even has to load itself into memory from the diskette and can load over your program which is held in RAM.

The ROM

Even so the DFS system is still very efficient in the use of Memory and releases a lot of diskette space that would otherwise have been used to hold the command files. The disadvantage of a ROM based system is that it is not at all possible to correct any errors that may exist in the DFS or update to a new version without replacing the ROM. As the ROM is not re-useable it must be thrown away. Therefore a lot of the DFS and Operating systems used in the B.B.C. Micro have been issued in EPROM. This stands for Electrically Programmable Read Only Memory. This type of memory chip is a semi permanent store. It has the ability to be erased through exposure to ultra violet light after which it can be reprogrammed again.

Using a DOS

This is still however an expensive business. The advantage of a DFS that is disk resident is that it is a lot cheaper to issue and is very flexible to alterations. The Disk based systems are usually called DOS. which stand for Disk Operating System. It can also be extended to become a sophisticated set of routines only being limited by the available space on the diskette. It is simply a case of issuing patch programs for the diskette to update the DOS. The obvious disadvantage of disk based DOS would be that it requires an area of memory to overlay its commands as and when they are called. As the normal Model "B" has only 32K to spare then it is not a bad idea to keep as much RAM free as possible.

Command syntax

All the DFS commands on the B.B.C. Micro are prefixed with a ★ symbol. An example of this is ★ACCESS ★BACKUP etc. All these commands normally have a default syntax to them and can be altered by extending the command to include such things as drive number <DRV>, filespec <FSP> and the directory <DIR>. Another extension is the partial filespec option known to B.B.C. Micro users as the ambiguous file spec or <AFSP>. That is to say that there are other alternative filespecs that will work. Examples would be ★ACCESS <AFSP> L where the <AFSP> can be a filename such as MYPROG.

Typing the command ★ACCESS ★.MY★ is also valid and would unlock any file of any directory on the current drive that begins with the letters MY. The files "W.MYPROG" and "A.MYLIST" would be included. Even though the two files are not in the same directory.

Filenames

When you are using a DFS based system then the SAVE, LOAD and CHAIN commands still work even though they are now stored and retrieved from disk. The only difference is in the speed of operation which is very much higher than cassette. Care must be taken also in the filename as you are limited to only 7 characters or digits or both. The reserved characters (# ★ . :) however must not be used as part of the filename. These characters have a special meaning to the DFS and could cause unpredictable results if not used correctly. Some DFS commands require the full filename to be used with them <FSP> and if they are not in the current directory then that must also be supplied.

Wildcards

Other commands will accept an alternative to the full filename

<AFSP>. This is normally a partial filename used with one of the Wildcard options. The Wildcard characters # and ★ may be used in the commands that have an <AFSP> attached to them. The # or hash stands for any single character and would indentify the file MYPROG and MYPROM using the Wildcard # in place of the last letter. Example MYPRO# would refer to both the files mentioned. The # can be used anywhere in the file name and simply means that any character in that position of the filename will be accepted as part of the filename. The other Wildcard option is the ★ or star. This stands for any group of letters and the above two files could also be called using MY★. This method should be used with care as all files that begin with MY..... will be referred to irrespective of how many characters are in the name. These Wildcard options are useful in the ★COPY ★WIPE ★ACCESS etc. The commands that take <ASFP> are given later in the book.

Full filespec

A full file specification would include the Drive number (1), Directory (2) and the Filename (3).

EXAMPLE
(1.).(2).(3......)
:1 . B . MYPROG

The complete filespec should always be enclosed in quotes. Although spaces have been included in the above line to highlight their order, there must not be any spaces or gaps in the filespec. Only the period or full stop should separate the different parts of the actual filename. This is the only way that the computer can tell the different parts of the filespec apart. If a drive number is included as part of the filespec then it must be preceded by a colon : . This allows the DFS to interpret the next part of the filespec as the drive number that it must refer to.

Directory spec

The Directory part of the filespec is a single letter that indentifies which directory it should refer to. The default directory is the $. on first power up. All the letters from A-Z can be used plus the $ sign. There can be more than one directory in a catalogue each divided by the prefix letter to the filename. The letter plus the period that precedes a filename is the directory that it belongs to. See also the CATALOGUE layout on page 21 Fig 6.1.

All the filespecs below are different for the reasons given.

":0.$. LANDER"
":1.$.LANDER"
":0.A.LANDER"

All the above refer to distinctly different files. The first refers to a file on drive 0, directory '$' that is called "LANDER". The second refers to a file called "LANDER" that is on drive 1 and the third "LANDER" although still on drive 0 is in directory A.

Default directory

The default or current directory does not show its assigned letter. Only when the directory is changed with the ★DIR (X) can the previous directory letter be seen. The DFS always starts in the $. directory of drive 0 but only when the directory is changed can the $. be seen in front of the filenames that it refers to. If the file that you require is in the current directory then you only need enter the filename or else you will have to enter the directory letter in front of the filename.

EXAMPLE.

"LANDER" refers to a file in the current or default directory but "A.LANDER" refers to a file in the 'A' directory.

Saving files

When saving files to the disk a full file specification is used even if you do not give it one. It would normally go to the default or current drive and be assigned to the current directory. If you were currently using drive 1 and were in the 'B' directory then saving a file like:–

SAVE "LANDER" would save it to drive 1 directory 'B' thus ":1.B.LANDER". If you wished the file to be saved on another directory then you should prefix the filename with the directory letter like SAVE "A.LANDER" would save it in the 'A' directory and if you wished it to go to another drive then you should use the drive number in the filespec like SAVE ":0.A.LANDER".

Chapter 8
The DFS Commands

Nearly all the DFS commands have an abbreviated form that they can be entered with. The ★ACCESS <AFSP> can for example be called up by just typing ★A. <AFSP>. At the end of the following command descriptions are given the minimum abbreviations i.e. (Abbr. ★.) that are needed to call the same command. Any abbreviation used must be followed by a period or full stop.

The following commands may overwrite memory and any current program should be saved before using the command. ★BACKUP, ★COMPACT, ★COPY,

The following symbols have special meanings and should not be used as part of the filename. (# ★ . :).

In this section of the book we shall list all the currently known DFS commands and their meanings.

★ACCESS <AFSP> (L)

This command locks a file against being written to. The purpose of this is to prevent accidental overwriting of a file by trying to save a file to disk of the same name as a locked file. It also prevents other commands such as DELETE, RENAME, WIPE and DESTROY from erasing the file. It is not however locked against format or backup. Only the write protect tab can prevent formatting and backup.

If you wish to save a file using the same name as a locked file then you must first unlock it. Typing the command ★ACCESS <FSP> will unlock the file whilst ★ACCESS <FSP> L will lock the file. <FSP> can be any valid filename. It is also possible to lock a file using the partial filespec with the wildcard option. ★ACCESS #.MY★ will unlock all files on the current drive whose name begins with the letters MY.

Covering the write protect notch of the diskette prevents all write operations to a diskette and will give the error 'Disk write protected' at any attempt to WRITE, SAVE, DELETE, RENAME, WIPE or DESTROY. The error message 'File locked' will be displayed if any of the above operations are attempted to a locked file even if the diskette is not write protected.

Abbr. ★A.

★BACKUP <Source drv> <Destination drv>

This command is for making a duplicate of a diskette. It must be enabled before it will work. If any errors occur after the enable stage then you must start again at the very beginning. The Source and Destination drive must be included in the backup command. Some examples are given below.

★ENABLE
★BACKUP 0 0

This is the command given to make a diskette duplicate using just one drive. It will alternatively prompt you for the source and destination diskettes until the complete backup is made.

★ENABLE
★BACKUP 0 1

Will copy the contents of the diskette in drive 0 to the diskette in drive 1. No prompts will be given. As soon as the second command line is given then the backup will commence.

Destination diskettes must have been already formatted or hold old data on them before they can be used. Failure to type the enable command in first will result in the error message 'Not Enabled'

Abbr. ★EN.
       ★BAC. <Source> <Destination>

★BUILD <FSP>

Will build a file of keyboard commands that can be executed directly from the file when it is run using the EXEC command. It can also be used to build the !BOOT file that is executed on auto boot. Example ★BUILD !BOOT. As each line is typed in it will be given a line number. At the completion of typing the build file, pressing the 'ESCAPE' key will transfer the file to the current drive.

A useful !BOOT file could for example define all your user keys upon power up. Each basic command to define a key would be typed on a separate line.

Abbr. ★BU. <FSP>

★CAT (DRV)

Will produce a catalogue of the diskette in the selected drive (DRV). Example ★CAT 1 will display the catalogue of drive 1. If no drive number is given then it will default to the current drive in use. The value for <DRV> must be in the range 0 to 3 and must be a valid drive in the system. If an invalid drive number is given then the error message 'Bad Drive' will be given. See section on explanation of diskette catalogue.

Abbr. ★. (DRV)

★COMPACT <DRV>

Example ★COMPACT 1 will compact the disk in drive 1.
This is a routine to tidy up any gaps in the disk catalogue and move all the free space to the end of the disk. If there are no gaps then this routine will not do anything. Gaps can occur when files on the disk have been deleted and have left gaps in the consecutive order that the DFS likes to write files. If the error 'Disk Full' is encountered it may well be than there is enough room on the disk but not all in one place. The compact command will find any gaps and move them into one continuous free area at the end of the disk. As the compacting takes place it displays file and block information to the right of the catalogue name of the file. These filenames will be displayed in the order that they are found on the diskette and not in their alphabetic order.

Abbr. ★COM. <DRV>

★COPY <Source Drive> <Destination Drive> <AFSP>

Routine to transfer a single file or group of files, when used with the Wildcard option, from one drive to another. EXAMPLE. ★COPY 0 1 MYPROG will copy the file 'MYPROG' from drive 0 to drive 1. And ★COPY 1 0 #.MY★ will copy all files on drive 1 whose filename starts with the letters 'MY' onto drive 0. Existing files on drive 0 will not be affected unless they have the same name and are not locked.
An efficient way to Backup a diskette and at the same time ensure there are no gaps would be the command ★COPY <SRC> <DEST> #.★. This would save having to ★COMPACT the diskette afterwards although the disk name and options would have to be added.

Abbr. ★COP. <Source> <Destination> <AFSP>

★DELETE <FSP>

This is used to remove any unwanted files from the current selected disk. EXAMPLE. ★DELETE MYPROG will search the catalogue for the file MYPROG and delete it from the catalogue. If the file is not found then the error message 'File Not Found' will be displayed. If the

29

file is locked then the error message 'File Locked' will be displayed and it will have to be unlocked using the ★ACCESS command first. Be warned that once the file is deleted it cannot be recovered. If the diskette is write protected then the error message 'Disk Write Protected' will be displayed.

Abbr. ★DE. <FSP>

★DESTROY <AFSP>

This is similar to delete except the Wildcard option may be used to remove a group of files.

The command must first be enabled via the ★ENABLE command otherwise the error message 'Not Enabled' will be displayed.

EXAMPLE. ★ENABLE

★DESTROY ★.MY★ will remove all the files from the current selected disk whose filenames start with the letters 'MY'. This would include MYPROG, MYLAR and MYSUMS. Great care should be exercised when using this command as the files cannot be recovered. All the files that match the Wildcard and will be removed are first of all displayed and the following question is displayed before they are finally removed. 'Delete Y/N?'. Only typing a 'Y' will result in the files being removed. After removal the message 'Deleted' will be displayed. Locked files will not be effected.

Abbr. ★DES. <AFSP>

★DIR (<DIR LET>)

This sets the current default directory. This is to say the directory that will be used in all loads saves. When the system is first turned or BREAK is pressed, it defaults to the .$ directory. The current directory is always displayed first in the catalogue listing. To load files from another directory you must prefix the filename with the directory letter.

EXAMPLES. ★DIR A will set the current directory to 'A'. If you wished to chain a file called W. CLOCK then you would have to include the W. of the filename but if you wanted the file A.BETA you could simply chain "BETA" as 'A' is the current directory. Any files Saved will now go to directory 'A'.

Abbr. ★DI. (<DIR LET>)

★DRIVE <DRV>

Changes the current default drive to <DRIVE>. All loads and saves will go to the default drive unless otherwise specified. ★CAT will catalogue the default drive. If another Catalogue is required then the drive number must be included in the command. <DRV> must be a valid drive number in the system otherwise the error message 'Bad Drive' will be given when an attempt is made to access it.

EXAMPLE ★DRIVE 1 will change the default drive to 1.
★CAT 0 will catalogue drive 0

Abbr. ★DR. <DRV>

★DUMP <FSP>

Will produce an hexadecimal listing of the file on the display. The file may now be listed and using control 'N' will enable it to be examined in the page mode. Control 'O' will turn the page mode Off.

Abbr. ★DU. <FSP>

★ENABLE

This is typed on its own without any parameters. It must precede the command ★BACKUP or ★DESTROY. If it is not given then the error message 'Not Enabled' will be displayed.

If any other characters are entered between ENABLE and BACKUP or DESTROY the whole sequence will have to be retyped or else the error message will be displayed again.

Abbr. ★EN.

★EXEC <FSP>

Executes the instructions line by line that are contained in the file <FSP> just as if they were being typed in from the keyboard. The ★BUILD command is used to write an ★EXEC file. This routine is useful if you have a sequence of keystrokes that you often use. One such sequence could be to define all the red user keys before using the micro. This command is also used to write the !BOOT file that is executed by holding down both the SHIFT & BREAK keys together then letting go of the BREAK key first. The effect of the !BOOT file is controlled by the OPT 4 X command covered later.

Abbr. ★E. <FSP>

★HELP (KEY)

The HELP command is used to get information about various

functions in the computer. If typed on its own will list out the ROMS fitted and the version numbers. It can also be used to get the syntax of the DFS commands or UTILS. It will not list out the main operating system commands ★RUN ★SPOOL ★SAVE ★EXEC & ★LOAD. This is because they are not part of the DFS ROM.

EXAMPLE. ★HELP DFS

```
DFS 0.90
  ACCESS <afsp> (L)
  BACKUP <src drv> <dest drv>
  COMPACT (<drv>)
  DELETE <fsp>
  DESTROY <afsp>
  DIR (<dir>)
  DRIVE (<drv>)
  ENABLE
  INFO <afsp>
  LIB (<dir>)
  RENAME <old fsp> <new fsp>
  TITLE <title>
  WIPE <afsp>
```

OS 1.20

And typing ★HELP UTILS will display

```
DFS 0.90
  BUILD <fsp>
  DISC
  DUMP <fsp>
  LIST <fsp>
  TYPE <fsp>
```

OS 1.20

Abbr. ★H. (Key)

★INFO <AFSP>

Will give all the information relating to the size, length and loading address of a file or group of files using the Wildcard option. This information cannot be found with ★CAT. If the file is not found then the error message 'File Not Found' will be displayed. The file information is displayed across the screen from left to right under the following headings.

32

Directory	File Name	Access	Load Address	Starting Address	File Length	First Sector
EXAMPLE ★INFO B. JOYSTK						
B.	JOYSTK	L	FF1900	FF801F	0000CB	08F

Abbr. ★I. <AFSP>

★LIB :(<DRV>).<DIR>

Sets the current drive and library. After this command the default drive and library will be those included in the command.

EXAMPLE ★LIB :1.B. This will make the default drive Drive 1 and the default directory 'B'. Any files saved will now go to this drive and be prefixed with 'B'. Typing ★JOYSTK would look on Drive 1 directory 'B' and if JOYSTK is found then it will be loaded and run just as if you had typed ★RUN :1.B.JOYSTK.

It is also possible to combine a utility program with a file on one command line. Suppose you had a utility program for printing labels and a file that holds your club members names and and addresses 'MEMADD' then you can print out the address labels using the line ★LABEL MEMADD where LABEL is the name of your label printing utility. This is possible because after the <FSP> any other text is stored in memory. A pointer to this is available for linking into machine code programs and anyone wishing to find more information on this subject should refer to the B.B.C. Users Guide page 454 onwards.

Abbr. ★LIB : (<DRV>).<DIR>

★LIST

Will display an ASCII text file complete with line numbers. Only those files stored as ASCII text or those made using the basic command PRINT # will be readable. It is also possible to list out the contents of a file made with the ★BUILD or ★SPOOL commands. It is not intended to list out BASIC programs with this command. As BASIC is stored in a compressed format it will not make any sense on the display. The BASIC program can be made into a text file by using the ★SPOOL command. Normal scrolling control keys CONTROL-N CONTROL-O and the SHIFT keys are used during the listing.

Abbr. ★LIST <FSP>

★LOAD <FSP> (ADDRESS)

Loads a file into memory using either the default address stored in the file or the address supplied in the command line.

EXAMPLE ★LOAD MYPROG

Will load the file MYPROG into memory at the address that it normally loads into memory whilst ★LOAD MYPROG 3000 will force the file to be loaded into memory starting at 3000. If the file is not found then the error message 'File Not Found' will be given. The filename may be enclosed in quotes but you must either use both quotes or none at all.

Abbr. ★L. <FSP> (ADDRESS)

★OPT 1 (n)

Will enable or disable a files information being listed on the display when it is being accessed. (n) is a 0 to disable or a non 0 (up to 99) to enable. For example if the enable is on then ★LOAD MYPROG will load the file MYPROG and then display the load address, start address & length etc. The syntax is given below. Either a space or a comma must follow or be inserted between the two values.

EXAMPLES. ★OPT 1,1 is the same as ★OPT 1 1. This enables the files loading information to be displayed. Whilst ★OPT 1,0 or ★OPT 1 0 will disable the files loading information.

Abbr. ★O.1

★OPT 4 (n)

Changes the setting of the auto start function of the default drive. There are 4 values for (n) 0,1,2 & 3. Each value represents a different way that the file !BOOT will be handled on auto start. That is after you have switched on and you press the SHIFT & BREAK keys together then release the BREAK key first. This is the way to invoke the auto boot. There must be a gap between the two values of OPT else the error message 'Bad Option' will be displayed. For a (n) value greater than 0 then the !BOOT file must be on the disk time of auto boot else the error message 'File Not Found' will be displayed. If the auto boot is selected then a file :0.$.!BOOT will be searched for. Finally the boot disk must not be write protected else the error message 'Disk Write Protected' will be displayed.

EXAMPLES of response to auto boot with different settings are.

★OPT 4 0   No auto boot action.
★OPT 4 1   Will ★LOAD the !BOOT file.

34

★OPT 4 2   Will ★RUN the !BOOT file.
★OPT 4 3   Will ★EXEC the !BOOT file.

Abbr. ★O.4

★RENAME <OLD FSP> <NEW FSP>

Renames a file to a new filename. It is also possible to rename the directory with it. It cannot rename a file from one drive to another. The file to be renamed must be unlocked else the error message 'File Locked' will be displayed. The disk must not be write protected else the error message 'Disk Write Protected' will be displayed. if the old filename does not exist then the error message 'File Not Found' will be displayed. Finally if the new filename already exists then the error message 'File Exists' will be displayed.

EXAMPLES

★RENAME MYPROG A.MYLIST
This has not only renamed the file but changed it from the default directory to the 'A' directory. If you do not wish to change directory then ★RENAME MYPROG MYLIST would have kept the default directory.

Abbr. ★RE. <OLD FSP>

★RUN <FSP>

Loads a machine code file, jumps to the start address and then runs it. The <FSP> can be preceded by a drive and directory. It does not run BASIC programs. Typing in the command ★<FSP> can be considered the same instruction that is to be run from the default drive and directory.

EXAMPLE.

★RUN :1.A.MYPROG
Will load and run the machine code file MYPROG from directory A on drive 1. ★RUN MYPROG will run the same file from the default drive and directory.

Abbr. ★R. <FSP>

★SAVE <FSP> <START ADDRESS> <END ADDRESS or LENGTH IN BYTES> (<EXECUTE ADDRESS>) (<RELOCATE ADDRESS>)

The command to save a machine code file or an area of memory to disk on the default drive and directory. This command is different to the basic SAVE command and should not be confused with it. The execute address and the relocate address may be omitted in which case they are assumed to be the same as the start address. The disk must not be write protected else the error message 'Disk Write Protected' will be displayed. There must be enough space on the diskette for the file or one of the following error messages will be displayed. 'Directory Full', 'Disk Full'. If the file already exists and is locked then the error message 'File Locked' will be displayed.

EXAMPLES.

★SAVE "MYPROG" SSSS FFFF EEEE RRRR

★SAVE "MYPROG" SSSS +LLLL

SSSS is a 4 digit hexadecimal memory location of the start address
FFFF is the 4 digit finish address
EEEE is the 4 digit execute address
RRRR is the 4 digit relocation address
+LLLL is the 4 digit length of the file that can be used in place of the end address.

   If it is used then it should be preceded with the + sign.

Abbr. ★S. <FSP> <START ADDRESS> <END ADDRESS or LENGTH IN BYTES> (<EXECUTE ADDRESS>) (<RELOCATE ADDRESS>)

★SPOOL <FSP>

Makes an ASCII or text file on disc of all the information on the display. Sends all subsequent output to the display also to <FSP>. The text for ★SPOOL can for example be a BASIC list program which is currently in memory. Simply give the file a name that is not in the current directory and use the following syntax.

★SPOOL <FSP>

This will open a file <FSP> ready to receive the text. Now type LIST and as the BASIC program is listed on the display it will also be written to the file named in <FSP>. The file must be closed afterwards with the command ★SPOOL. This will correctly close the file <FSP> and terminate spooling. It can be called again from the ★LIST ★EXEC or ★TYPE commands. The BASIC listing that is in <FSP> is not stored the same way as a normal BASIC program. This is because a normal BASIC SAVE command saves the program in a compressed format.

Abbr. ★SP. <FSP>

36

★TITLE <DISK NAME>

Writes the master disc name of the current default drive. The name can be up to 12 characters long and if all 12 are not used then it fills the remaining characters with blanks. Any characters may be used. The name must be enclosed in quotes.

EXAMPLE

★TITLE "UTILITY 2"
Will give the disk the name UTILITY 2 and three blanks will be added to the end of the name. The name can be changed as many times as is needed. The disk must not be write protected else the error '**Disk Write Protected**' will be displayed.

Abbr. ★TI. <DISK NAME>

★TYPE <FSP>

Will display an ASCII or text file on the screen that has been created with the ★BUILD ★SPOOL or BASIC PRINT# similar to ★LIST but without the line numbers. As with the ★LIST command this is not intended to display a BASIC program stored in compressed format.

EXAMPLE.

★TYPE MYPROG
Will display a listing of the text file saved and under the <FSP> MYPROG. Normal scrolling keys Control–N and Control–O are used with this command.

Abbr. ★TY. <FSP>

★WIPE <AFSP>

Carries out a controlled purge of specified files or group of files. The file names are displayed and queried as to whether they should be erased. After deletion the catalogue is rearranged. Once the files are erased they cannot be recovered.

EXAMPLE.

★WIPE ★.MY★
Will offer MYPROG and MYLIST from any directory. Answering 'Y' to any filespec displayed will erase it. Pressing any other key will keep the file intact.

Abbr. ★W. <AFSP>

Diskette Utility

★VERIFY (<DRV>)

Diskette verification program (Acorn utilities). Although verification is carried out during format there are times when a diskette may give read errors. If no number is given for the drive or the (<DRV>) is omitted then it will use the default drive. ★VERIFY (<DRV>) will examine each and every sector on the diskette for readability. If it finds any unreadable sectors then it will terminate with an error message and the track that the error occurred on. If it verifies successfully then it will display each track number as it is read.

Abbr. ★V. (<DRV>)

Chapter 9
Random Text Files

Besides the obvious gain in speed of access a disk based system has over cassette tape, there are some program areas that a disk based system comes into its own. One of these is in the handling of Text Files. This is even more true in the handling of Random Access Files. These are files that can be written in data form onto the diskette. It then allows you to retrieve just the bit of data you require, without the need to search all the way through sequentially until you get to it. The latter would be the case of the cassette tape method. With the DFS system however you can set the PTR# to point to the position in the file that you wish to write or read.

Buffer

When reading or writing Random Access files an area of memory is set aside for this purpose. It allocates 256 bytes to the area and this area is called the Buffer. All communication to or from the diskette must go through this Buffer. As it happens, each sector on the diskette is exactly 256 bytes and therefore the Buffer is used to hold one sector's worth of data. If you are reading a file each sector is loaded into the Buffer as it is required. If you are writing to a file then as the Buffer is filled it will write the complete Buffer contents to the next sequential sector and ready the Buffer for another 256 bytes of data. The Buffer will also transfer its data to the sector if the file is closed using the 'CLOSE#' command.

Open Buffers

It is possible to have more than one Buffer open at the same time. You may for example wish to read from one Buffer and write back through another. The B.B.C. Micro allows up to five Buffers to be used or, put another way you can have up to five files open at the same time. The reader is strongly advised to read the B.B.C. Users Guide where a reasonable explanation is given on normal file handling. Also described are the basic keywords:–

OPENIN. Opens a file for data input.

OPENOUT. Opens a file for data output.

OPENUP. Opens a file for updating. (This command is only available with the new BASIC ROM.)

INPUT   X. Inputs the next block of data from the Buffer X.

PRINT   X. Outputs the next block of data to the Buffer X.

BGET   X. Gets one byte of data from the Buffer X.

BPUT   X. Outputs one byte of data into the Buffer X.

EOF   X. Gives a value of (−1) if the end of the file has been reached or a value of (0) if it has not been reached.

To check if you have the BASIC with the OPENUP command simply type the command 'REPORT'. If you get the message:

(C) 1982 Acorn

then it is almost certain that you have this command. If you get an earlier date, then this command is not present. Another way to find out if it is present is to simply type the command on its own. 'OPENUP' if present will simply return a Syntax Error whilst if it is not available will give the message Mistake.

Open command

The additional keywords PTR# & EXT# are related to disk filing and will be explained here. A lot of the commands used in a Tape based system are exactly the same in the Disk environment, although they may mean slightly different things. The 'OPENOUT' command opens a file for writing. It checks the catalogue for the file name. If it exists and is not locked then it is used. The length of the existing file is used to calculate the number of sectors allocated to the file. If it does not exist then an entry is made into the catalogue and 64 sectors are reserved for the file. This is important to remember as you may already have a fairly full diskette and be surprised to see the error 'DISK FULL' or other alternative message appear. A lot of space is required for the 'OPENOUT' command with a new file name and 64 sectors means 6 tracks and four sectors. On a 40 Track diskette that is just over one sixth of the diskette. The thing to remember is that if you do not use all 64 sectors then only the space required for your file is taken from the diskette in the 'CLOSE #' statement.

Larger files

It is possible through a few programming tricks to allocate more than 64 sectors if that amount of space is required. Please remember that for every 2560 bytes or 10 sectors, a complete track is used.

100 X = OPENOUT "ADDRESS" will open a file for output in the current drive of the current directory called 'ADDRESS', where X is equal to a currently assigned variable.

If the file name already exists it will be used and the file length will be that already allocated. If the file name does not exist then a catalogue entry will be made for the file named 'ADDRESS' and will be used by this file only. In the latter case if there are not 64 free consecutive sectors then an error message will be displayed and the program terminated.

Pointers and extents

If this is a new file then the values for PTR# and EXT# will be 0. The keyword PTR# will always point to the next location of the file that will be read or written to. It always points to the last location used plus 1. The EXT# will return the length of the file. On a new file both these commands point to the same area. As the file is dynamically increased so the PTR# and EXT# will move together. When the file is completed and saved through the 'CLOSE #' command then the EXT# will always point to the extent of the file. Thus when you issue the command:–

100 X = OPENIN "ADDRESS", after a successful load the PTR# will point to the start of the file and the EXT# will point to the end of the file.

End of file

Another command used here would be the EOF#. This command is normally used in a test to see if the end of file has been reached. It can be used as part of a FOR NEXT loop:–

200 IF EOF#X THEN 2000
2000 CLOSE#X

Or it can be used as part of a REPEAT UNTIL command:–

200 REPEAT
210 ....
220 ....
230 ....

41

240 ....
250 UNTIL EOF#X
260 CLOSE#X

Both of the above statements mean the same. When the end of file is encountered then close the Buffer assigned to the variable X.

Sample

In the following program each Data Element has 7 bytes allocated them and will produce space for 50 entries of 5 lines with each line having room for 7 letters and spaces.

```
100 X = OPENOUT "TESTING"
110 FOR Z = 1 TO 50
120 PRINT #X,"SPACE 1"
130 PRINT #X,"SPACE 2"
140 PRINT #X,"SPACE 3"
150 PRINT #X,"SPACE 4"
160 PRINT #X,"SPACE 5"
170 NEXT Z
180 CLOSE #X
```

And here is a simple program that will read the contents of the above file back.

```
100 X=OPENIN "TESTING"
110 REPEAT
120 INPUT #X,TEST$: PRINT TEST$
130 UNTIL EOF #X
140 CLOSE #X
```

Run the two programs and see just how much data has been stored. In the first program the data stored could easily be the result of an INPUT statement. Prior to each file entry being stored, two further bytes are added to the front of entry. (See fig 9.1). These two bytes reference the type of data being used and the length of the entry to be stored. Therefore even though all our entries were the same length at 7 characters each, the PTR#X moved 9 places for each entry. Each record then occupied five of these entries.

Recalling Records

This should be taken into account when recalling specific file entries. For example if you wanted record number 3 then you would calculate the PTR # X on the following basis. There are seven data bytes plus two identifier bytes for each line entry. This makes nine bytes per row. There are five rows per record thus each record is five rows times nine bytes long. Simple maths now shows that each record is forty five bytes long. Therefore 3 ★ 45 = 135. Making the PTR # X = to 135 would then point to the start of the third record.

Pointing

To recap, when calculating the next position for PTR # X, 2 bytes must be added for each entry. Thus for the above program 7 bytes would be used for data storage and two for the data type and length. PTR # would be moved either in groups of nine to get to specific line in a record or it would be moved in groups of forty five for each complete record. The next program shows how to go directly to the third record as discussed above.

```
100 DIM TEST$(50)
110 X=OPENIN "TESTING"
120 PTR # X=135
130 FOR Z = 1 TO 5
140 INPUT # X,TEST$
150 IFEOF # X THEN 200
160 PRINT TEST$
170 NEXT Z
180 PRINT EXT #X
200 CLOSE # X:END
```

Note that we can find out the total length of the file at anytime by asking for the extent or EXT # X as in line 180. If you have followed the examples then you should get an answer of 2250 for EXT # X. The second point to remember is that each time an entry is read then the PTR # X is moved to the start of the next entry.

Data mark

The first of the extra two bytes that precede the data indicate what type of data is being stored and the other byte is used to indicate the length of the data. The data type is one of three types. A hex value of 00 would indicate it was a string type followed by the length. A value of 40 hex would indicate the data was an integer value and would be followed by 4 bytes that contained the integer. Finally a hex value of FF would indicate the data was a real number with the following 5 bytes containing the number. The diagram below shows how the

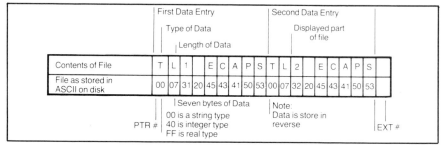

	First Data Entry							Second Data Entry						
	Type of Data							Displayed part of file						
	Length of Data													
Contents of File	T	L	1	E	C	A	P	S	T	L	2	E	C	A	P	S
File as stored in ASCII on disk	00	07	31	20	45	43	41	50	53	00	07	32	20	45	43	41	50	53

Seven bytes of Data
00 is a string type
40 is integer type
FF is real type

PTR #

Note: Data is store in reverse

EXT #

Figure 9.1. A typical file that is open to read two data entries.

data is stored in the file. Note that after the data type and length each element of the data is stored in reverse. All blanks are padded out to the next data type marker.

Disk space

Always exercise great care when running with 3 or more files open. Some of the keywords like ★LOAD ★SAVE ★EXEC ★SPOOL ★BUILD ★LIST & ★DUMP will try to use some of your work area variables. Should you open more than one file at the same time with new names then each file could take up to 64 sectors making a total of 128 consecutive sectors. If you require more than 64 sectors for your file then you will have to devise a way of pre allocating space for the file.

One way would be to write a dummy file of the length you wish the file to be. Then when you open the file a second time you can overwrite it with the valid data.

```
100 X = OPENOUT " ADDRESS "
110 FOR Y = 1 TO 250
120 PRINT # X, "LENGTH FOR NAME"
130 PRINT # X, "LENGTH FOR ADDRESS"
140 PRINT # X, "LENGTH FOR TOWN"
150 PRINT # X, "LENGTH FOR COUNTY"
160 PRINT # X, "SPACE FOR POST CODE"
170 NEXT Y
180 CLOSE # X
```

Note that in the above program each line is of different length and should be taken into account when writing your program to calculate PTR # X for reading the file back or making entries into it. The program also demonstrates how a large file can be built up with dummy data. In this case we wanted to reserve space for 250 names

44

and addresses. This meant that each record was allocated just 90 bytes. The total number of sectors used can be calculated by the number of bytes times number of entries and divided by the sector length of 256. This gives us an answer of 88 sectors after rounding the answer up to the next integer.

The data in the dummy file will be overwritten by the real data when the file is used.

Practical program

We can now show a simple practical program that will use the above saved data space.

```
10 ON ERROR GOTO 210
20 A=0:R=0
30 X=OPENOUT "ADDRESS"
40 PRINT "RECORD NUMBER";R :REM RECORD STARTS AT 0
50 PTR #X=A : REM A KEEPS THE PTR # IN SYNC
60 INPUT "(1) TO ENTER DATA OR >(2) TO END";ENTER
70 IF ENTER >2 THEN 210
80 INPUT "FIRST LINE OF TEXT";L1$
90 PRINT # X,L1$
100 INPUT "SECOND LINE OF TEXT";L2$
110 PRINT # X,L2$
120 INPUT "THIRD LINE OF TEXT";L3$
130 PRINT # X,L3$
140 INPUT "FOURTH LINE OF TEXT";L4$
150 PRINT # X,L4$
160 INPUT "FIFTH LINE OF TEXT";L5$
170 PRINT # X,L5$
180 A=A+90 :REM KEEPS RECORD LENGTH TO NINETY
190 R=R+1 :REM NEXT RECORD NO.
200 GOTO 40
210 CLOSE # X:END
```

If the above program has already been used once, then a second access to it can be made using the 'OPENUP' command.

And a program that will actually read the data put in with the above program.

```
10 ON ERROR GOTO 130
30 X=OPENIN "ADDRESS"
40 INPUT "RECORD NUMBER OR >50 TO END";R
50 IF R>50 THEN 130
```

```
60 R=R★90: REM KEEPS PTR ⁴ X IN SYNC
70 PTR # X=R
80 FOR L = 1 TO 5
90 INPUT # X,LI$
100 PRINT LI$
110 NEXT L
120 GOTO 40
130 CLOSE # X:END
```

Reserving diskette space

Another recognized way to allocate a lot of file space is to use the
★SAVE command and use the length parameter with it to specify the
file length. Let us assume that you have calculated that you wish to
reserve 24k byte of data area. Simply give the file a dummy name and
save it with a length of 24k (although the hex value will be needed).
As it happens 24576 in decimal rounds very nicely to 6000 hex.
Therefore the following command will reserve all your space.

★SAVE "ADDRESS" 00000+6000

You will find that until you actually start to write to the file the
contents will be random characters or garbage. Always remember
that a lot of diskette space is required for this type of exercise.

Chapter 10
Catalogue Address Byte Layout

It was stated that the B.B.C. DFS stores the program name and retrieval information in the first two sectors of the diskette. The actual bytes for each sector can be summarized as follows.

Sector 0 byte:–

00 to 07. Store the first 8 bytes of the disk title. The second part is stored in the next sector making the 13 locations reserved for the title.

08 to 0E. This is the first filename followed by the letter of the directory at 0F.

10 to 17 Are the filenames of the second catalogue entry followed at location 18 by the directory letter. This procedure is continued for a total of 31 catalogue filenames.

Sector zero print out

See Figure 10.1 for an actual print out of the first two sectors.

The first characters preceding the colon are the relative sector byte. This is followed by the actual hex listing in each line with an ASCII representation of what it means. If there is no ASCII equivalent of the character then a period or full stop is printed instead.

It is therefore very easy to see that the bytes from 00 to 07 go to make up the first eight letters (of the 13 character) title. This diskette has the title 'Utility'. If you check them against an ASCII list you will see it is just that. But remember that the title is 13 characters long and if all 13 are not used then they are padded out with blanks.

First filename

The Bytes 08 to 0E contain the first filename 'KEYBD   '. Here you can see that because we did not use all seven available characters allowed in the file name the last two positions were padded out with blanks. The last character at byte 0F is the directory for the file and it is the 'W' directory. The next line starting at byte 10 gives the next

```
                                SECTOR Ø

000000:  5574 696C 6974 7900 4B45 5942 4420 2057   Utility.KEYBD    W
000010:  4443 4F4E 5620 20A4 5645 5249 4659 20A4   DCONV   .VERIFY .
000020:  464F 524D 3830 20A4 464F 524D 3430 20A4   FORM80  .FORM40 .
000030:  2142 2020 2020 2024 4249 4F52 5448 4D57   !B      $BIORTHMW
000040:  5048 4F54 4F20 2057 504F 454D 2020 2057   PHOTO   WPOEM    W
000050:  5048 4F4E 4520 2057 4241 5442 414C 4C57   PHONE   WBATBALLW
000060:  4D55 5349 4320 2057 434C 4F43 4B20 2057   MUSIC   WCLOCK  W
000070:  2142 4F4F 5420 2024 4845 4C50 2020 2057   !BOOT   $HELP    W
000080:  5041 5454 4552 4E57 4B49 4E47 444F 4D57   PATTERNWKINGDOMW
000090:  4249 4F20 2020 2057 4D45 5353 4147 4557   BIO     WMESSAGEW
0000A0:  4250 4152 5432 2057 414C 5048 4120 2057   BPART2 WALPHA   W
0000B0:  4341 4C43 2020 2057 534B 4554 4348 2057   CALC    WSKETCH W
0000C0:  4B45 5942 4420 2057 494E 4445 5820 2057   KEYBD   WINDEX  W
0000D0:  636F 6E74 656E 7424 5745 4C43 4F4D 4557   content$WELCOMEW
0000E0:  0000 0000 0000 0000 0000 0000 0000 0000   ................
0000F0:  0000 0000 0000 0000 0000 0000 0000 0000   ................



                                SECTOR 1

000100:  0000 0000 28D8 3190 0019 1F80 4604 CD4C   ....(.1.....F..L
000110:  0019 1F80 C901 014A 0028 0028 0002 0148   .......J.(.(...H
000120:  0028 0428 0003 0145 0028 0028 0003 0142   .(.(.(.E.(.(...B
000130:  0019 1F80 BA02 013F 0019 1F80 1E19 CD25   .......?.......%
000140:  0019 0019 0010 0115 0019 1F80 B125 00EF   .............%..
000150:  0019 1F80 E11B 00D3 0019 1F80 0F08 00CA   ................
000160:  0019 1F80 F304 00C5 0019 1F80 0808 00BC   ................
000170:  0030 0030 0B00 00BB 0019 1F80 2B01 00B9   .0.0........+...
000180:  0019 1F80 1507 00B1 0019 1F80 6622 008E   ............f"..
000190:  0019 1F80 B019 0074 0019 1F80 FE03 0070   .......t.......p
0001A0:  0019 1F80 C002 CC6D 0019 1F80 8011 005B   .......m.......[
0001B0:  0019 1F80 8A14 0046 0019 1F80 9D07 003E   .......F.......>
0001C0:  0019 1F80 FE24 0019 0019 1F80 990A 000E   .....$..........
0001D0:  0000 0000 B003 000A 0019 1F80 D407 0002   ................
0001E0:  0000 0000 0000 0000 0000 0000 0000 0000   ................
0001F0:  0000 0000 0000 0000 0000 0000 0000 0000   ................
```

Figure 10.1.

file name followed by the directory. This process is repeated for the rest of the sector giving a total of 31 entries.

Sector 1

Sector 1 contains in the first five bytes the remainder (if any) of the diskette title. That is where the similarity with sector 0 ends. Bit format is used at some locations. That is to say that the bit pattern for the byte is obtained and various bits are either used independently or added to other bytes and make longer words.

The rest of the information is used as follows:–

Byte 05 is the number of entries in the catalogue multiplied by 8.

48

Byte 6 is used in bit format. Bits 0 & 1 are high order bits of the next byte (07) which go to make a ten bit word. Bits 4 & 5 are the !BOOT start up option as set with OPT4,X.

Byte 07 plus the 2 high order bits of byte 06 go to make up a 10 bit number that stores the total number of sectors on the diskette.

This has taken up the first half of line 0. The second half of line 0 plus the 8 bytes in each half of the rest of the sector give the actual information relative to a file name in the exact same half of a line in sector 0. The first file starts its address at:–

Byte 08. This is middle order bits of the files load address.

Byte 09. The low order bits of the files load address.

Byte 0A. The middle order bits of the files exec address.

Byte 0B. The low order bits of the files exec address.

Byte 0C. The middle order bits of the files length.

Byte 0D. The low order bits of the files length.

Byte 0F. In bit format. Bits 0 & 1 are used with the next byte to make a ten bit number. Bits 2 & 3 are the high order bits of the files load address. Bits 4 & 5 High order bits of the files length. Bits 6 & 7 High order bits of the files exec address.

Byte 0F preceded by the first 2 bits of byte 0E give a 10 bit number. This is the starting sector number on the diskette for the file.

This process is repeated for rest of the 31 available catalogue entries for the files.

Address bits

As can be seen above, the LOAD, EXEC & LENGTH are stored in two bytes plus 2 bits of another byte. As there are 8 bits in each byte this gives a total of 18 bits for each of these entries. The 2 high order bits are used to address another I/O processor if they are set to 1. It can also be seen that the bits are not stored in consecutive order.

Only the first 8 bytes of sectors 0 & 1 contain information about the disk. The second 8 bytes and all following groups of eight bytes contain file information. The filename in sector 0 has its storage information in exactly the same bytes of sector 1.

Chapter 11
DFS Error Messages

The B.B.C. Micro has an extra system numbered of error messages that can be displayed as a result of the machine not being able to complete part or all of a procedure or finding a bad syntax. In the early DFS these were displayed in HEX format and the user should refer to this list for their meaning. In the newer DFS then you are more likely to be presented with the full error description rather than a code. The most common error reported is Disk Fault 18 at YY/ZZ. Refer to error C7 for explanation of this.

BD = NOT ENABLED.
Some commands such as the ★BACKUP and ★DESTROY should be preceded with the ★ENABLE command. This code means that ★ENABLE was missing or overwritten.

BE = CATALOGUE FULL.
An attempt was made to store more than 31 files in a catalogue. Either change to a fresh diskette or ★DELETE files to make room. Can also be presented as Disk Full.

BF = CAN'T EXTEND.
Insufficient space at the end of a Random Access file to extend it any further.

C0 = TOO MANY FILES.
An attempt was made to open more than the allowed five files at any one time.

C1 = FILE READ ONLY.
Write attempted to a file opened for read only.

C2 = FILE OPEN.
An attempt was made to open an already open file before it was closed or the ★BUILD, ★DELETE or ★SAVE commands were issued to a file which was open for data access.

C4 = FILE ALREADY EXISTS.
This error will be displayed if you try to rename a file to another existing filename. Can also be displayed as Bad filename.

C5 = DRIVE FAULT XX AT YY/ZZ.

This usually refers to a disk drive hardware fault and an examination of the drive and/or media is required. See C7 for XX, YY & ZZ details. Can also be displayed as Drive fault.

C6 = DISK FULL.

It means just that. There is not enough room left on the diskette to save your program or to open a file for output using the OPENOUT # command.

C7 = DISK FAULT XX AT YY ZZ.

Means there is a fault in trying to read or write to the diskette. The fault code is at XX. The track is at YY and the sector ZZ. This could mean a media fault, non formatted diskette, drive door open or any number of combinations that prevent the computer accessing the diskette. In simple terms the computer was unable to find the sector/track. It could be that for some reason the diskette has become corrupted. Normally it simply says Disk fault.

C8 = DISC HAS BEEN CHANGED.

Whilst a file was open the diskette used in the open file has been removed or exchanged for another diskette.

C9 = WRITE PROTECTED.

The diskette has a write protect tab fitted and an attempt was made to write to it. More likely to say Disk read only.

CA = CHECKSUM ERROR.

The control block and checksum of each open file is held in memory. This error would normally mean that the data has been corrupted.

CB = ★OPT OUT OF RANGE.

An invalid number was used with the ★OPT1 or ★OPT4 command.

CC = INVALID FILENAME.

The wrong filespec syntax or number of filespec characters was exceeded. Now displayed as Bad filename.

CD = BAD DRIVE NUMBER.

Either the drive is not ready or in the system or a drive number greater than :3 was used. Now displayed as Bad drive.

CE = BAD DIRECTORY.

Error in specifying the directory. Either the wrong character or number of directory characters exceeded 1.

CF = ★ACCESS SYNTAX ERROR.
The wrong letter was used with the ★ACCESS command. The only letter allowed to be used with this is 'L' which stands for LOCK. Now displayed as Bad attribute.

D6 = FILE NOT FOUND.
The named file was not found in the current drive or directory.

FE = WRONG COMMAND SYNTAX.
The DFS did not understand the command given to it. Perhaps part of the command was missing like placing a '★' before a system command. Most likely to appear as one of the following messages:– Bad Command, Mistake, No such variable or Missing".

Disk faults

It is now more likely that you will be presented with a description of the fault rather than a code. It is possible that a code could be presented with the message as with Disk fault 18 at YY/ZZ. Other codes (XX) that might appear with the Disk fault XX are 16 Write fault, 14 could not find track 0, 10 Drive not recognised or ready and errors 08 to 0E are to do with CLOCK, DMA and CRC checks.

Unless you really know what you are doing, please do not open the case of the B.B.C. Micro.

Contact one of the many B.B.C. service centres now set up.

Chapter 12
Technical notes on the B.B.C. Micro

On the front right hand side of the keyboard are a number of holes that may be linked to alter the way the Micro responds to various active and invisible commands. These links are numbered from left to right and those relevant to this book have the following meanings.

Links 3 & 4. These are to adjust the track to track stepping rates. They should not normally need to be touched and unless you are sure that you know what you are doing then DON'T touch them. In the case of TEC standard drives which step at 6m/s link 3 should be made and link 4 should be unmade. With the 80 track drives which step at 3m/s then both links should be made. Do not forget that if you have switchable 80 track drives then the step times are doubled in the 40 track mode and the links should be set to accommodate this. If you are unsure of the stepping rate of your drives then these two links should be left unmade. Trying to use the faster access times on drives that are not designed to step fast can cause damage to the drive.

Link 5. This determines the start up sequence. Normally after you switch the computer ON then you will press the 'BREAK' key to initialize the resident filing system. If you press 'SHIFT & BREAK' together (releasing 'BREAK' first) this will enable you to run any !BOOT program on your diskette, provided the ★OPT4 has been set. With link 5 made simply pressing 'BREAK' on its own will initiate the start up option if it is set.

Double sided drives

Underneath the keyboard there are some other links on the main PCB. The most important one of these is at the left hand front corner. It is marked S4 and has three solder terminals. The centre terminal must be linked to the outermost terminal (that is the terminal on the left) for correct operation of Double Sided Drives. If this link is not made it will not allow access to the other side of the diskette and all references to Drives 2 & 3 will go to Drives 0 & 1 respectively.

This link does not affect the operation of Single Sided Drives.

55

Catalogue faults

A strange fault can appear on the B.B.C. Micro when you issue the command for the catalogue. This is when the catalogue header shows, but nothing else. It might give you the impression that the diskette contains no files at all. There are two possible reasons for this associated with all P.C.B. issues but which require different cures.

Early P.C.B.'s

On the B.B.C. Micro the main P.C.B. has undergone a number of revisions and all P.C.B.s that are marked ISSUE 3 or less have to have a small modification carried out around IC27 and S9. This modification requires pin 9 of IC27 to be lifted from the P.C.B. A short wire is then taken from this lifted pin across to the right hand side of link S9. The track that runs from the right hand side of S9 back to the now vacant pin 9 hole of IC27 should be cut.

Later issues

On ISSUE 4 P.C.B.s and later it is quite often found that link S9 is made. It should be cut for proper DFS operation and correct catalogue display.

Should you be unable to get your Micro working properly always check the following points:–

● Are all plugs and sockets fully home in their respective connectors?

● Are any of them damaged?

● Is the power getting to all units on the system?

● Have you got the correct software settings in the options?

If DFS problems then check the following:–

● Have you got the correct diskette for your machine? An example would be are you trying to load a friends 80 track diskette on your 40 track drives?

● Did you shut the drive door?

● If the drive rotates then is the diskette corrupted? Remember the purpose of keeping a backup!

● If this is the first time used then has your machine got the COMPLETE Disk Upgrade?

● Did you follow ALL the unpacking and installation instructions paying particular attention to the DIL Switch Assembly?

Chapter 13
The Switchable Drives

One of the more popular type of drive now appearing on the market is the Switchable drive. This is normally an 80 Track drive with modifications done to the stepper motor circuit. These have appeared in all drive sorts and sizes. There are full height drives, $^2/_3$ height drives and half height drives.

The odd one out

The $^2/_3$ height drive is an oddity in that the natural progression of drives has been from full height to half height. As in most modern computer applications things are normally done in the ratio or base of two. That is to say double the memory size, double the disk capacity and so on. Therefore it is only natural that if something for the computer is to be reduced in size then $^1/_2$ would seem like the correct sum. Somehow the $^2/_3$ height crept in somewhere along the line and and is an oddity.

It is unfortunate that the above sum cannot be applied to the price of the drive.

Switching down

The main purpose of the switchable drive is to enable the user of an 80 Track system to READ software or diskettes that have been recorded on a 40 Track drive. It is NOT recommended that you use the switchable drive to write or make a forty track diskette for use in a standard forty track drive.

Track width

Chapter Two gave the different track pitches for both 40 and 80 Track drives. From this it is found that the 80 track drive lays down its tracks over the same area as the 40 track drive. Therefore the 80 Track drive has a track thickness of exactly half that of the forty track drive and a correspondingly smaller gap in the Record - Playback head. It is because of the different track widths that the 80 track drive can get inside the track bands of the larger 40 track drive. The reverse is however not true. If you use one of the switchable drives to make a forty track diskette you will be making it with narrow track widths and the 40 track drive head will overlap not only the track it is supposed to read but also the intertrack guard band plus part of the next narrow track. See figure 13.1 for a diagram of these effects.

Possibilities

If you have no option but to attempt to make a 40 track diskette on a switchable drive then you are more likely to have success if the diskette to be used is first Bulk Erased with a proper magnetic erasure. The other alternative is to use brand new diskettes that have not yet been used or formatted.

Precautions

When using the drives in the forty track mode be very careful not to run programs that will take the head beyond the natural end track of the diskette. This can be done for example by running the 80 Track formatter whilst in the forty track mode. Extreme damage can be done to the head carriage assembly if this is allowed to happen. At a minimum it is possible to force the alignment of the drive beyond its specification and the only alternative will be to return the drive for service.

Maintenance

When used correctly then all quality drives will give years of reliable service. This is also true of the switchable drive. There is only minimum maintenance required and that is to keep them clean and after any heavy period of use run a head cleaner diskette. The head cleaning kits available should only be used when you feel it is absolutely necessary to do so. Make sure that the diskette is well drenched in cleaning fluid before inserting it into the drive. DO NOT leave the cleaning diskette rotating in the drive for longer than 15 seconds. That is all the time needed to clean the head/s. Any periods of greater than fifteen seconds can result in the diskette drying out sufficiently to become abrasive to the delicate head/s of the drive. Keep head cleaning to a minimum and certainly not more than once in three months.

Keep out rubbish

Always take time to examine your diskettes at regular intervals. Inspection of this kind can often find a potential candidate for the scrap bin before it shows up and destroys some valuable software. In particular look for scored rings or pits on the diskette. Always

58

examine diskettes that have been given to you by another party, before committing them to your drives. Try not to use the drives in a dirty or dusty atmosphere. When possible DO NOT use unbranded diskettes or those of unknown origin. By using branded diskettes you can be sure that the manufacturer has had the confidence to put their own name on the diskette box and label. Simple precautions like this can lead to years of untroubled service from your drives.

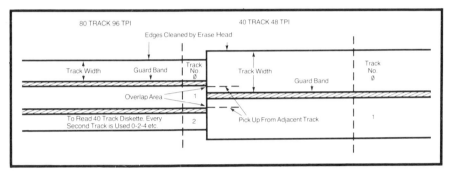

Fig. 13.1. Here it can be seen that the 80 track drive can read inside the 40 track width, but the 40 track read will overlap into the adjacent tracks of the 80 track drive.

Chapter 14
Half Height Drives

During the early chapters of this book we covered the correct setting up of the Link or Drive select setting of a typical TEC Floppy Disk Drive.

As there are a number of other types of drive available, it was felt that an extra chapter on the setting of some of these drives would be helpful to those people who had purchased them. In particular, I will cover the correct setting for some of the following half height drives: TEAC and MITSUBISHI, plus the earlier full height TEAC.

The drives offered by these companies vary from the standard 40 track single sided drive to the 80 track Double sided drive. In the case of the MITSUBISHI drive, which is also one of the types chosen by ACORN for use on the B.B.C., it is an 80 Track Double Sided drive.

This is currently the only type of drive made by MITSUBISHI. Whilst they have plans to extend the range, at the time of writing the new models are not available.

Head loading

With the TEAC drives, they employ a head load solenoid. This means that it requires either a Motor On or a valid Drive select signal before the head can be loaded against the media for communication with the diskette. This is the purpose of the two switch or link options found on most drives, HM or HS. These stand for Head to Motor and Head to Drive Select respectively. That is to say in the first instance, with the link set to HM, the head of the disk drive will be loaded against the diskette media any time the motor is started up. It may well be that the computer wishes to access another drive, but as all the Motor On lines are usually connected together on the SA400 system, the motors of all the drives on line will be activated. Thus any drive that has the HM option set will load the head of that drive against the media. When the computer comes to use that drive, then the drive will already be in a condition to pass information to and from the diskette.

Head to select

With the switch or link set in the HS position then the loading of the head against the media will only take place when that particular drive is actually selected for communication between its diskette media and the computer. That is to say that with the HS option selected and a drive set to be drive one or DS1 of the system, then only when drive one is selected will the head of the drive actually be loaded ready for use.

For and against

There are arguments for and against both methods of head selection. With the HM option there is more wear on the diskette due to the head always being loaded when any drive on the system is selected or used. Any disk drive "LOAD" or "SAVE" command will load all the heads of all the drives on the system whether they will be used or not. Any drive access however small will result in all the heads of all the drives being loaded against the media.

With the head select in the HS position the head of a particular drive will only be loaded when the drive itself is selected for use. That is to say that if drive zero or DS0 was being used, then the head of drive one or DS1 will not be loaded against the media. With the HS option it can be seen that the drive head is only loaded when it is actually required to communicate between the computer and the diskette of that drive.

Settling time

The arguments go like this. If you have the HM option selected then the drives will not require a Head Settling time before the drive is Ready for use. It speeds up drive to drive access time for certain and is a lot quieter if a lot of drive to drive transfers are taking place. It also means that the diskettes are subjected to greater wear due to the longer time that they are left in contact with the drive head.

In the case of the HS option then diskette wear is reduced to a minimum as the head is only loaded against the media when an access is required to THAT particular DRIVE. This results in a lot of clicking taking place during drive to drive transfers, as the heads are selected only when they are needed. It also means that when the drive is selected then a small amount of time must be allowed for the head to settle against the diskette before access is attempted to the diskette. This is what is known as Head Settling time and can be as much as 50 m/s in the older type of drive.

Self loading

It may be that you have come across a drive that does not contain either the HS or HM links or switches. If this is the case then your drive is most likely similar to the TEC drives whereby the head is loaded against the diskette every time the drive door is closed. This means that the head of the drive is in contact with the diskette at all times. Even when the drive is stationary. This results in a higher degree of diskette wear than a drive with the HM option set. There is also the likelihood of the diskette being corrupted if the power is removed from the drive whilst the diskette is still inside it. The advantage of the non solenoid drive is that it is quite a bit cheaper to buy and there is less to go wrong. It is one of the factors to consider when purchasing a drive for any computer. Having said that, it is always recommended that diskettes should NOT be left in any drive when it is not in use. The safest place for a diskette is in the protective sleeve it was supplied in. It is also good practice to only insert the diskette after all the system is turned on and remove the diskette first before any of the system is turned OFF.

Multiplexing

Another connection that can be found on Floppy Drives is the MX link or switch. This is the one that causes most trouble and confusion. Its purpose is to allow two or more drives to be connected together on the same cable. Incorrect setting of this connection can have the most surprising results. It can even cause you to think that there is a fault with another drive on the system.

The right way

Reference to chapter three of this book shows that in the TEC drives the MX link is normally in the unmade position. This is the normal way for this link to be set. With the older TEAC full height drive the MX switch tends to operate in the opposite sense and prefers to be in the ON position. That is to say the MX is normally OFF or unmade for multiplexing two or more drives. TEAC have now corrected this anomaly and all the current half height drives will require this link to be unmade for correct operation. It has also been found that this link can be (and normally is) left unmade, even on a single drive system.

Drive select

With the new type of drives, the drive selection remains the same as with the previous full height drives. If you wish the drive to be the BOOT drive or ZERO drive then you will make the link DS0. If you wish the drive to be drive one then you will make the connections DS1. Reference to Figure 2.4 will show that the B.B.C. uses the opposite side of the diskette for drives two and three. This only applies if the user has purchased double sided drives. Users of the B.B.C. should not attempt to make connections DS2 or DS3. Only one of the Drive Select (DSx where x = a value 0 to 3) switches should be made for any drive. No two drives on the same system should have the same Drive Select switches made.

Another terminator

As in chapter three page 10, ALL floppy drives need to have the drive cable terminated with a resistor. Only one resistor should be on the entire system. Normally it is left in the last drive on the cable. These resistors are now appearing in different colours and forms. In most drives they can be identified easily by looking for what looks like an unusually shaped DIL package that is located in a socket. The unwanted terminators can then be unplugged or removed.

Fixed terminators

With the MITSUBISHI drives a different system is used whereby the terminator is fixed within the P.C.B. of the drive. With this type of terminator it is necessary to remove a number of links that connect the terminator into circuit. Figure 14.1 shows a typical link setting for the MITSUBISHI drive. It can be seen that the drive is set to be the BOOT drive or DS0 with the HS option for the head to load only when access is required to that drive. No MX link is made. Whether the drive be used on its own or with another on the same system, this link will be left unmade.

Different links

Just above these links and to the left is the fixed resistor pack that is the terminator. As it is soldered into the P.C.B., the row of links just below it are all removed to take it out of circuit when required. No other links should be adjusted or tampered with as damage to the drive can result.

Figure 14.2 shows the correct setting for a TEAC slimline drive.

64

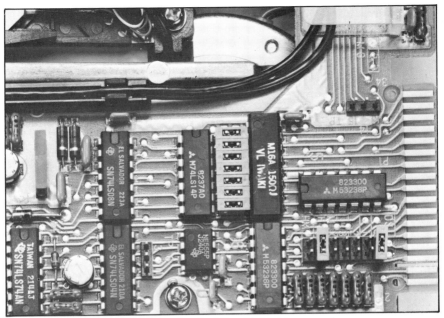

Figure 14.1. Typical link setting for the Mitsubishi drive.

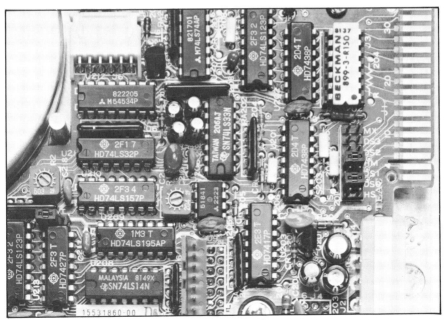

Figure 14.2. Correct setting for a TEAC slimline drive.

65

Note the different locations of the links and indeed the different order that they are laid out. The drive is again set to be a BOOT drive or DS0. The white "BECKMAN" resistor pack can be clearly seen. It is this pack which serves as the terminator and is simply unplugged on drives that do not require their use.

Rounding off

In the final example Figure 14.3, the switch settings for the full height TEAC are shown and the drive is set to be drive one. It can also be seen that the HS option is used as stated earlier, the MX switch is forward. The terminator resistor is located just in front of the switch assembly and is white in colour. This can be removed if there are other terminating resistors in the system. If you require the Head to Motor option (HM) then the DIL switch assembly is unplugged and moved one space to the left. This will allow you to then set the HM option although you will have to reset the other switches as they will no longer be in line. If you wanted the drive to be the BOOT drive or drive 0 then the following switches will be placed forward:– DSO,

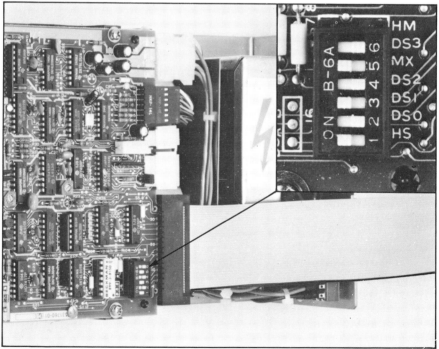

Figure 14.3. Setting the DIL Switch.

MX and HM. An easy way to tell if the switch settings on these drives are correct is that three switches must be forward and three switches must be towards the back of the drive.

Final comments

If you are unsure of what to do then always get expert advice. Most manufacturers including CUMANA supply the drives already addressed and with the correct resistor terminator. There is normally no need to open the unit or make any adjustments unless you wish to add other drives to the system. Before making telephone calls for technical advice please read all the literature supplied with your drives, as most answers can be found there. Also read the technical notes in this book. They have been placed there as a result of answering many queries.

Appendix 1
Utility Diskette for the BBC

As ACORN only supply a UTILITY diskette when the complete Disk Drive is purchased through them other, reputable Disk Drive Suppliers will provide a Format and Verify Diskette at nominal cost. Always ensure that the disk formatter you purchase is the vendor's own copyright or one that he has an agreed copyright to and not an ACORN copy. If you are supplied with the latter through any other source than the official ACORN channel then you will be in infringement of copyright.

The Cumana Disk Formatter, for example, is sole copyright of Cumana Ltd and is supplied with an understanding that the original user can make as many copies as he/she wishes provided that these copies are not made for financial gain or benefit.

The original user is also permitted to make as many copies of the operating instructions of the Cumana Ltd Disk Formatter provided that he/she again does not do so for financial gain or benefit. The formatter is supplied in good spirit and to promote self education at home, club and school level.

Because of the freedom given to the use of this diskette Cumana Ltd will deal with any fraudulent use of the diskette program or instructions very severely. So be warned.

To make your own Utility Diskette it is simply a matter of getting your "WELCOME" cassette and transferring the programs from Tape to Disk. This is done by typing ★TAPE and then loading the first program on the tape, (not the tape setting program). After it is loaded type in the command ★DISK or ★DISC either spelling will do. Now type SAVE"proname" and ensure that the program name is not more than seven characters long. List the program and find the line that calls the next tape program. It will read CHAIN "". For diskette use the "" will have to contain the name that you will give to the next program transferred from tape. Before transferring the "PHOTO" program obtain the info on the address by performing ★OPT1 2. Use this information to ★LOAD the file and after calling the DFS ★SAVE it back again. This is because this file has a small amount of machine code tucked into it. It can be made easier by offsetting the load address to a more useful area. Try the following steps. RESET the computer before proceeding.

1/ ★TAPE
2/ ★LOAD"PHOTO" 4000
3/ ★DISC
4/ ★SAVE"PHOTO" 4000+9F4 E00 8000

You will find that you can now run it under the normal CHAIN command from diskette.

This simple method will then be almost identical to the real thing. All you have to add is your Cumana Formatter and Verify Program.

To make the Diskette "Auto Boot" simply use the ★BUILD command to create the file which chains the first program.

If the first program that you wish to run on "Auto Boot" is the Welcome program then simply follow these steps:–

★BUILD !BOOT
00010 CHAIN"WELCOME"
00020 press ESCAPE key.

Note that the line numbers are automatically put in for you and on line 00020 simply press the ESCAPE key to cause the file to be written back to the diskette.

Now type ★OPT4 3. This will set the 'Auto Boot' to load and run the file '!BOOT' every time the 'SHIFT/BREAK' method is used to "Auto Boot".

Appendix 2
Programming with the DFS

When programming on a machine that has the DFS fitted it should be remembered that its lowest memory location used for LOMEM is Hex &1900 or 6400 Decimal. This is different to the Tape version of the B.B.C. Micro which uses a different LOMEM of Hex &E00 or 3584 Decimal. This means that the DFS machine has 2816 bytes less than the tape version. If you wish to run tape programs on a DFS machine then it can be put into the tape mode by issuing the command ★TAPE. It still however leaves LOMEM at &1900. Normally this is no problem and most tapes will run as is. The exception to this would be a very long tape program. In this case it will be necessary to issue the command LOMEM = 3584. This will then completely restore the 2816 missing bytes for use down at &E00.

Tape onto disk

The other problem comes when programs are transferred from Tape to Disk. Nearly all reasonable length Basic programs will transfer by issuing the command ★TAPE then Loading the program from tape. Now issuing the command ★Disc and Saving the program will store it onto diskette.

Some other programs are more difficult to transfer because they will not run from diskette due to them needing to load over this Disk workspace.

Moving down

The way round this problem is to get the program to load at the current PAGE (&1900) and move it down in memory. One of the most popular ways to achieve this is by programming one of the function keys to do the job for you.

The program given finds the TOP of the current program and sets up a for next loop using PAGE as the start address and TOP as the end address. It then transfers the program down by 2816 bytes, resets PAGE then restores the program to run. The pling (!) operator could have been used to move 4 bytes at a time but it was felt that the program would be easier to understand if we used a single byte transfer.

★KEY0 FOR X%=PAGE TO TOP:?(X%−2816)=?X%:NEXT: PAGE=&E00¦M OLD¦M ★TAPE¦M RUN¦M

Now all you have to do is to Load the program from diskette and press the F0 button. This will then relocate your program down at &E00 and run it.

Be warned though, if you press the BREAK key then the pointers will be moved back to the DFS area and you will have to start again.

Reserved locations

When writing directly to memory there are certain locations additional to those given in the USER GUIDE that should be avoided as these may conflict with the DFS or Floppy Disk Controller. The Floppy Disk controller occupies the addresses from &FE80 to &FE84. It is in the same area as the VIAs, CRTC, ULA's, ADLC and A to D. This area is part of the Sheila allocation and goes from &FE00 to &FEFF. In general all locations above &8000 are dangerous areas to write to and unpredictable results can occur.